Mary Mitchell November,
1972

BARRE PUBLISHERS · BARRE, MASSACHUSETTS · 1972

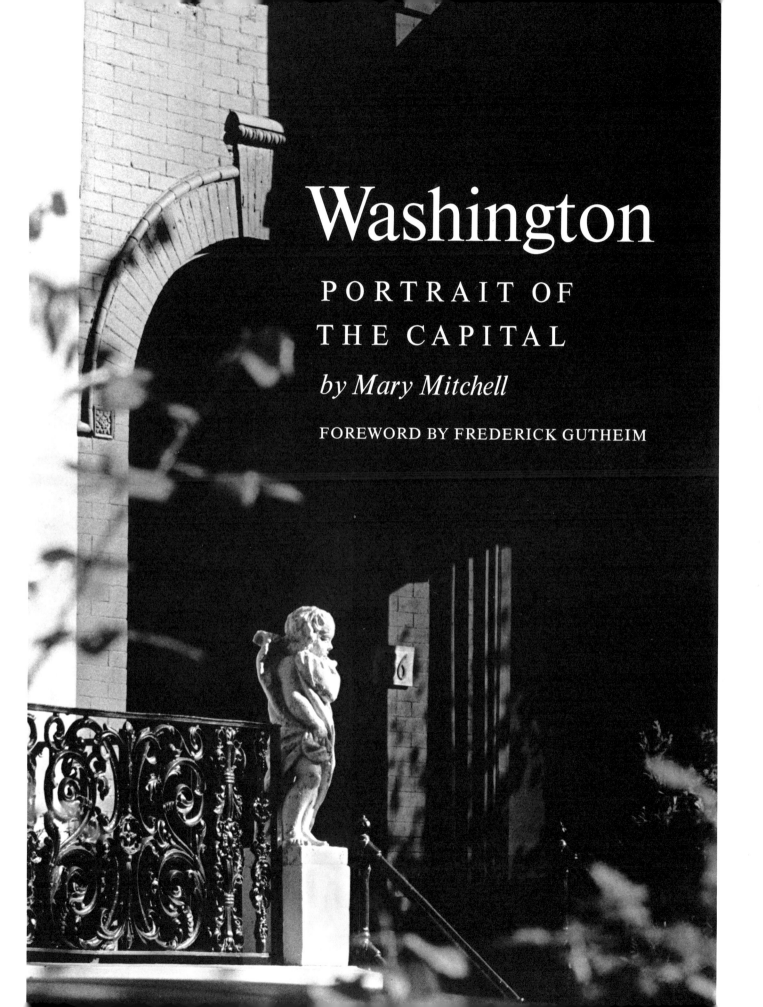

Washington

PORTRAIT OF
THE CAPITAL

by Mary Mitchell

FOREWORD BY FREDERICK GUTHEIM

ACKNOWLEDGMENTS *are due friends who kindly became companions, and my patient family who cooperated as chauffeurs and weekend bodyguards. Especially I thank proprietors of Little Caledonia, Rive Gauche, and The Monocle who courteously allowed me to photograph inside their shops and restaurants. I also thank Orlando Gault and Duane Mansley and the reliable, competent crew at Allen Photographic Service for help—even on Sunday. My gratitude also goes to Thomas de Kun for his expertise in the darkroom, and the help of his able assistant, Umbi Singh.*

Library of Congress Catalog Card Number 72-83229
International Standard Book Number 0-8271-7222-2
Designed by Klaus Gemming, New Haven, Connecticut
Text set by Finn Typographic Service, Inc., Stamford, Connecticut
Printed by The Meriden Gravure Company, Meriden, Connecticut
Manufactured in the United States of America

TABLE OF CONTENTS

FOREWORD

THE visual discoveries of Mary Mitchell's Washington are the product of diligent searching, not accidents of the lens. Here are quietly arranged appointments with flowers in bloom, sunlight, rain-soaked pavements and other carefully anticipated or awaited moments. Such a juxtaposition as the Lincoln Memorial, the striking appearance of a towering black man—and his appearance on ice skates—has not been contrived; but in a creative sense it was prepared for, and the moment seized when it appeared.

Cities have been witnessed by many photographers, from Atget to Weegee. What Mary Mitchell offers is not the introspection of the studio, or the crashing shock of the news headline, but the quietly seductive observation to which one willingly returns and thought-fully contemplates. Her photographic art is informed by a love of mankind, historical discipline and what can best be described as a certain urban loyalty. But it is also a matter of arising early, getting out in all kinds of weather, and acceptance of the risks of a single woman at work in a hard part of town, and at an odd time of day. Her book on Georgetown first showed these characteristics.

The Washington described here, however much it is historically determined, is certainly the modern version of the national capital city. The views of Thomas Jefferson are still consulted before a decision on height zoning is taken. But it is also host to nearly 20 million tourists a year, and home for the very old, for swinging singles, for the politically engaged, and the very poor in one of the fastest growing metropolises in the land. The population of central Washington is also predominantly Black—although this share of the total has not changed significantly since Civil War. Mary Mitchell has not sensational-ized this aspect of the city, but offers a balanced and reasonable view.

Here then one is offered a honest view. One is introduced to the less familiar but significant parts of the city—the national arboretum, the gardens of Dumbarton Oaks, the chateau country of Kalorama, the canal tow path. It is a view populated with interest-ing people, planted tastefully with trees, shrubs and flowers. It is presented as one would hope to find it—a city of all seasons.

To commend this thoughtful view is to offer hours of rich enjoyment for both the mind and the eye, historical insights and visual satisfactions. This urban environment, its judicious blend of the monumental and the everyday, of architecture and landscape, of past and future, will bear revisiting. And I believe it will meet the test of time, a document the future will examine with profit and enjoyment when much else that now attempts to describe the city of Washington must be acknowledged a failure.

Frederick Gutheim

Washington, D.C.

PREFACE

In March 1791 Pierre L'Enfant stood on the hill which was to become Capitol Hill, facing west. He saw a plain with swampland around a tidal creek, and hills surrounding the plain like an amphitheatre. In the distance, as the Potomac River narrowed on its inland course, there was a harbor where a former colonial town named Georgetown thrived as a tobacco port.

With the French passion for formalizing the landscape, L'Enfant envisioned a mall reclaimed from the swamps and stretching to the River. A street-grid would align the plain, and superimposed on this, wide avenues would radiate across the city from central circles, as spokes from the hubs of wheels.

Today this tremendous design is a reality, in the main, as the Frenchman foresaw it. The grid brought order. A century later the lowlands were controlled and became a setting of beauty.

After twenty years of living here and recently, after almost three years exploring the area, I find that abundant, authentic evidence of the past survives, making this modern, important city all the more vivid and exceptional.

Mary Mitchell

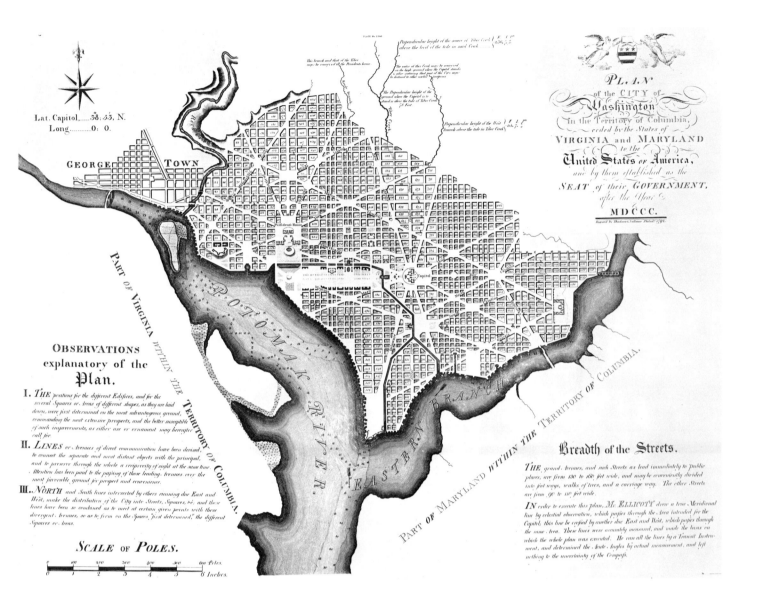

Ellicott's Map of Washington 1792 — Philadelphia Plate (engraved by Thackara & Vallance of Philadelphia). On August 18, 1791, Thomas Jefferson asked Pierre L'Enfant and the surveyor Andrew Ellicott to make a map of the federal territory. He wrote:

> If you do I would suggest to you the idea of doing it on a square sheet to hang corner upwards, thus the outlines being N.W. N.E. S.E. & S.W. the meridian will be vertical as they [*sic*] ought to be; the streets of the city will be horizontal and vertical, and near the center, the Potomac and Eastern branch will be nearly so also; there will be no waste in the square sheet of paper. This is suggested merely for your consideration.

For reasons of his own, L'Enfant did not carry through with the suggested engraving. But Ellicott did. His map, based on L'Enfant's plan, became the official map of the new capital, and was circulated on the eastern seaboard and in Europe to promote the sale of real estate in the United States capital.

1 *The White House, Lafayette Square and down Seventeenth Street to the Pan-American Union . . .*

This book will take you into many out-of-the-way places, some just across from the beaten path. Here for example, is a fountain thirty feet away from where visitors to the White House queue up. Sparrows love it but tourists scarcely look at it. It is dedicated to Archibald Willingham Butt, long-time and devoted aide to Presidents Theodore Roosevelt and William Howard Taft, who went down with the *Titanic* April 15, 1912.

Leaving through the north doorway, you depart with a vivid sense of history and the surprising intimacy of the public rooms. The garland was on the original design of the Irish architect James Hoban, of 1792.

Opposite: "The White House is where all the magic is," wrote a sixth-grader. At almost any hour, day or night, you can find people looking through the grille and reacting like this young girl.

The south Portico added in 1824 was the original front entrance until 1829 when the North Portico was built and the entrance reversed. Harry Truman liked to step out onto a back porch for a breath of cool summer air at night, and he added the second floor balcony. The only casualty was the back of the $20 bill. The plate had to be redesigned to include the porch.

Alexander Hamilton was first Secretary of the Treasury. But there is another good reason for his standing there on the Capitol-White House axis, facing the Potomac. He participated in the famous Residence-Assumption Bargain which seated the federal government where it is today.

In the spring of 1790 Thomas Jefferson returned from five years in Paris as American Minister to become Secretary of State in George Washington's cabinet. Two issues were dividing Congress. One was the assumption of the Revolutionary War debts of the newly established states by the federal government. Promoted by Hamilton, it was opposed by the southerners led by the Virginians. The other was the site of the infant nation's capital.

Uninvolved because of his long absence, Jefferson nevertheless wanted to see the conflict resolved, and in June invited the New Yorker and his two leading opponents, Richard Bland Lee and Alexander White, congressmen from Virginia, to dine with him and try to reach a reasonable settlement. Over fine French wines, Hamilton promised northern votes for a Potomac location, and in return the Virginians agreed to change their votes to support his funding bill. The first instance of log-rolling in the annals of Congress, the bill was enacted July 16, 1790.

Facing north, is Albert Gallatin, second Secretary of the Treasury (1801–1814). Like Hamilton he was not a native American. Hamilton was born on the island of Nevis in the British West Indies, and Gallatin in Switzerland.

Right: Across The Avenue from the White House, Andrew Jackson on his perfectly balanced steed has been doffing his hat to the President ever since 1853. *Below:* Lafayette Square in early spring.

A wintry day near St. John's—Lafayette Square, built in 1816
by the English architect, Benjamin Henry Latrobe.

Thomas Jefferson was fortunate he did not have to see this cupola on the crossing of St. John's while he was in the White House. He disliked cupolas on classically designed buildings. Latrobe, who was Superintendent of the Public Buildings during Jefferson's two terms as President, argued that that cupola not only gave a finished look but was also a practical method of ventilating the roof. When Latrobe suggested adding a cupola to the low rounded dome designed for the Capitol by William Thornton, Jefferson would not allow it. Sixty years later, it was indeed added, and now what would that great dome be without it!

Opposite: Madison Place reflections.

The Count de Rochambeau, general of the French Army who helped Washington bottle up Cornwallis at Yorktown, stands on a pedestal pointing toward the Executive Offices. In the near background is the handsome row of restored antebellum houses on Jackson Place. In the far background, the dark red brick of a federal building. The Square has an air of detachment and the antebellum past found nowhere else in monumental Washington, and provides a pleasing, tranquil setting for the White House.

Opposite: On the opposite corner at 748 Jackson Place, is the Stephen Decatur House which was designed by Latrobe in 1818, and the first house built on the Square. Erected and lavishly furnished with prize money he had earned from fighting the Barbary Pirates in the Mediterranean, Commodore and Mrs. Decatur only enjoyed it for a single year. On March 22, 1820, a week after giving a brilliant ball celebrating the marriage of Maria, President James Monroe's daughter, he met Commodore James Barron on the duelling ground at Bladensburg, Maryland, and was brought home through the wide hospitable door to die in the arms of his wife Susan.

William W. Corcoran had James Renwick, architect of the Smithsonian, design this splendid example of Second Empire French architecture for his art gallery in 1859 at Seventeenth and Pennsylvania. But then along came the Civil War, and the Quartermaster General took over the rooms so elegantly outfitted in puce and tasseled decor. After the war the Gallery moved to new quarters, the handsome classical gallery further south on Seventeenth Street. It had become by 1970 a "crumbling eyesore," with sooty façades, grimy garlands and chipped festoons. Now under the Smithsonian's auspices it emerges again as the Renwick Gallery, decorated as of 1859.

When Admiral David Glasgow Farragut won fame at the Civil War battle of Mobile Bay, with his slogan: "Damn the torpedoes. Full steam ahead!" he naturally could not know how prophetic his order was. The Metro will soon roll full steam ahead underneath his cannon-decorated pedestal. Dedicated in 1881, this attractive little urban park in the heart of Washington's business center has seen modern office buildings replace all the Victorian mansions which once adorned its streets.

Strolling down Seventeenth Street with pink magnolias in
bloom at the west entrance to the Executive Offices.

What is this photographer doing, his back to the handsome lion of the Corcoran Art Gallery and ignoring the wedding-cake architecture of Old State?

Throughout the mid-nineteenth century there had been intermittent talk about resettling the capital in the Mississippi Valley. But when Congress allocated funds during Grant's first administration for the erection of this monstrous French Renaissance pile to house the State, War and Navy Departments, the question was settled once and for all. Washington was the capital.

By the Thirties all departments had outgrown the building. Too expensive to tear down, it survived. By 1943 the Pentagon was finished for the Defense Department, and State occupied the whole. When the new State Department was at last finished by 1960, this building was then adapted later as the Executive Offices.

This statue of Queen Isabella of Spain was given by the Spanish government to the Organization of American States, which is located in the Pan-American Union Building at the corner of Seventeenth and Constitution Avenue. It is where "the obstinate Mr. Burns," as George Washington called him, had his cottage. Burns refused to sell his fertile land to the new and untried United States government for a capital city. So the President, a shrewd and long-time dealer in real estate himself, started the survey at the other end of the Ten Mile Square, at Carrollsburgh, as if Burns' land wasn't valuable. It didn't take long for the Scotsman to come round. He was second on the list of proprietors to sign the agreement on March 29, 1791, offering his land for sale.

2 *Along F Street to the Lincoln Memorial and Georgetown . . .*

Before the British burned the White House on August 24, 1814, President and Mrs. James Madison escaped into the country. They returned in a few days to occupy the Col. John Tayloe house at the corner of New York Avenue and Eighteenth Street, known today as The Octagon, headquarters of the American Institute of Architects. On this table in Madison's second-floor study, on February 17, 1815, the President ratified the Treaty of Ghent, ending the War of 1812 with Great Britain. The nail-studded strong-box was that in which Henry Carroll brought the Treaty to Secretary of State Henry Clay.

This red brick mansion at 1801 F Street, built in 1802, and looking surprisingly compatible in its glass and cement setting, has seen more dramatic action than the sale of Easter bunnies littering the opposite corner. During the Civil War sheds and corrals occupying open land between Eighteenth and Twenty-Second Streets and sheltering over a thousand horses, caught fire December 27, 1861. Hundreds were burned, and the rest stampeded all over the vicinity, and toward the River and Georgetown.

Above: Walking west on F Street you encounter the substantial urban complex of George Washington University. Founded in 1821 on Meridian Hill outside the City's boundary as Columbian College, it moved to mid-town Washington in the early Eighties. In 1904 it moved over to Foggy Bottom and was named George Washington University in order to distinguish it from Columbia University in New York City and to honor the first President. *Below:* The University has kept up a continuing interrelationship with people in public and urban affairs and international relations. The seminar on foreign relations which W. Averell Harriman gave in the winter of 1971–2 is typical of what students here can find.

Skating on the Reflecting Pool of the Lincoln Memorial is a sport few visitors to
Washington can ever enjoy, for the weather has to remain cold long enough to develop
a four- or five-inch crust before the Park Department will allow skating. Once on the
ice, however, some demonstrate skills like this expert caught in a spin at 1/500th of
a second.

Children warming hands at fire in a barrel.

Above: Late afternoon light of early March on the fountains at the Pool's east end. *Left:* One way to descend a flight of steps. *Opposite:* About thirty years before Daniel Chester French carved the Lincoln figure, he had done the statue of Dr. Thomas Hopkins Gallaudet, the great teacher of the deaf, showing a child how to fingerspell the letter A. In 1921–22 when French was pondering how to do Lincoln's hands, he remembered this earlier experience. Here Lincoln's left hand spells the letter A for Abraham, and the right hand, out of the picture, spells the letter L.

Opposite: Another memorial to another assassinated President. A red carpet extends the full length of the 630-foot grand foyer at the Kennedy Center of the Performing Arts. Eighteen crystal chandeliers given by Sweden light the foyer and the tall, floor-to-ceiling windows. High up, against the window-wall, is the rough-textured, bronze head of the unmistakable man for whom the center is named. The sculptor was Robert Berks.

The fishermen are setting their lines near the intersection of 26th and G Streets at the edge of Georgetown harbor. Here in June, 1801, was a wharf with stone warehouse belonging to Tobias Lear. At this wharf were berthed schooners from Philadelphia which had brought down the boxes of government papers, archives, and furniture to establish the infant government in the new capital.

Today Rock Creek is a shallow stream between Washington and Georgetown. But in the Federal era, enough water flowed to accommodate eight small mills upstream and ocean-going vessels.

In the early eighteenth century Georgetown flourished as a tobacco port for planters of southern Maryland at the head of navigation of a great river reaching far into the hinterland. Canny Scotsmen with names like Magruder, Gordon, Peter and Dunlop soon arrived to found an export-import trade so successful that the colonial Maryland commissioners ordered a town platted in 1751 to be called George-Town. By 1789 the new United States Congress named it an official port of entry with a customhouse. The growing government needed more housing, and southerners settled here to become federal clerks. With a way of life structured around slavery and inherited wealth, they imbued the town with a "southern" flavor which persists to this day.

By 1871, the coming of steam navigation, the competition of railroads, and the growth of the capital, combined to toll the bell for Georgetown's commercial importance. Losing its charter, it became part of the city of Washington. For fifty years it remained an unfashionable, but pleasant and quiet neighborhood, gradually adding to its housing base by building small row houses here and there for people who found living here convenient and inexpensive. When the New Deal of the Thirties and then World War II brought a demand for more housing, Georgetown became a desirable address. Concerned citizens, some of them descendants of the original settlers, struggled against aggressive commercial interests to retain the town's integrity and its harmonious blend of Federal and Victorian architecture. Meeting this challenge has meant an unremitting but successful struggle. In 1967 Georgetown was declared a National Historic Landmark. You can sense the special character of this historic red brick town on the Potomac so different from anywhere else in Washington.

Above, left, right: Shopping mall, country market, Foire Gastronomique, Venetian Rialto, where you can find Caneton a l'Orange and cheeseburgers, handcrafted sandals and *duck presses,* Mexican rebozos and *Batik* skirts, antiques—the axis of Wisconsin Avenue and M Street.

Above: Duck a l'Orange at Rive Gauche, Washington's oldest and one of the most select French restaurants. Its site at the southwest corner of M and Wisconsin is that of George Gordon's tobacco inspection house built before 1750.

The barge drawn by mules and now run by the National Park Service recalls the times when barges brought grain, furs, and coal down from the interior on the Chesapeake & Ohio Canal, and returned up the Canal as far as Cumberland, Maryland with products from east coast ports. The Canal was built between 1828 and 1850, and ceased business operation in 1924.

A tranquil summer morning on the old towpath, now maintained from
Georgetown to Cumberland by the Park Service for hikers and bicyclists.

Georgetown is noted for its charming but secret gardens. Only the owners, visitors on a garden tour, or neighbors tending their own backyard gardens penetrate to the rear from streets almost solidly fronted with houses built close together.

Memorial plaque near the door of the old Vigilante Fire House on Wisconsin Avenue.

Odalisque in an O Street garden.

The steeple of Christ Episcopal Church looms high above this row of old houses on Dumbarton Avenue. If you're in this neighborhood around noon, you will hear the carillon at Christ Church ringing the changes of the hour.

Opposite: Walking home along P Street after church.

Georgetown University's incomparable silhouette just above Key Bridge is one of Washington's loveliest skylines. It was founded in 1789 by Archbishop John Carroll, a Jesuit with an unerring eye for a building site.

Opposite: Begun around 1800, this famous mansion has over the years been altered or added to by many successive owners, but found its fulfillment when the Hon. and Mrs. Robert Woods Bliss bought it in 1922 and began to build its unusually beautiful gardens. They worked with an intimate friend, the noted landscape gardener, Mrs. Beatrix Farrand. Enthusiastic collectors and world travelers, they gradually assembled a magnificent collection of Byzantine art, a unique and select Byzantine art reference library of 40,000 volumes, and a rare Pre-Columbian collection. In 1940 they deeded Dumbarton Oaks to the President and Fellows of Harvard University complete with collections, library and furnishings.

In 1944, the mansion became the scene for an international conference from which emerged the beginnings of the United Nations.

The Pre-Columbian collection was smaller but equally fine, and had been at the National Gallery of Art. But after Robert Bliss died in 1962, bequeathing his collection to Dumbarton Oaks, Mrs. Bliss had Philip Johnson, the architect, design a museum for it. Johnson's building is situated in a heavily planted area where its contemporary architecture of glass and stone would not conflict with the Federal style of the brick mansion itself.

Left: A little boy thinks a cherub is for drinking, not for looking. *Below:* An eighteenth-century French terra cotta sphinx guards the doorway from the Orangery to the gardens.

Laid in the former tennis court, the Pebble Garden is a dramatic composition of baroque designs. Especially striking is the sheaf of wheat made of amber-colored stones. The Bliss crest bears this design, and the motto Quod Severis Metes (As Ye Sow, So Shall Ye Reap). By looking carefully while in the gardens, you can spot the sheaf used in many ways, as finials on wrought-iron gates, or in the stonework.

3 *Along Massachusetts and out into the old County . . .*

A buffalo guards each side of the bridge crossing Rock Creek between Georgetown and Washington on Q Street. In the background on the corner of 23rd and Sheridan Circle (1606 23rd Street), is the Turkish Embassy, built originally in 1912 by Edward H. Everett of Vermont for 220,000 dollars, an excessive price for that era. Everett, a pioneer in the glass industry, invented the bottle-cap.

This mansion was undoubtedly one of the triumphs of the architect, George Oakley Totten, Jr., graduate of the Ecole des Beaux Arts in Paris, who built more embassies than any other architect, and four around Sheridan Circle.

Here at 2020 Massachusetts lived Evalyn Walsh McLean whose "Father Struck It Rich" in 1896 in Ouray, Colorado, at the Camp Bird gold mine. This lavish mansion is now the Indonesian Embassy whose handsome red and white flag enlivens Massachusetts Avenue every day west of Dupont Circle. Sometimes the Indonesian Embassy staff forms a "Gamelan" or orchestra to entertain a group, in this case, the Metro-Washington Wellesley Club.

The Phillips Gallery, at 1600 21st Street, installed in the former home of the family for which it is named, is unique in its atmosphere of informal comfort. Here a visitor looks at Edouard Manet's "Ballet Espagnole." On the right is a Corot, "View from the Farnese Gardens," and left, "The Stonebreaker" by Georges Seurat. This rich collection specializes in the French Impressionists, and in another building adjacent to the house, are several of the more famous Cézannes, Renoirs, and Van Goghs.

Built by Mrs. Richard Townsend, the wife of a railway magnate, in 1900, this mansion at 2121 Massachusetts now belongs to the Cosmos Club whose members are noted scientists and scholars. Before moving here the Club had its headquarters at the old Dolly Madison House on Lafayette Square.

Embellished by rambler roses piercing the wrought iron fence of the Cosmos Club, this corner of Massachusetts is also the beginning of Florida Avenue. Until 1890 Florida was known as Boundary Street, the limit of the city of Washington as laid out by Pierre L'Enfant.

After 1890 when Washington outgrew its old boundaries, the area around this Circle was platted and Sheridan Circle named for the great Civil War cavalry leader, Lt. Gen. Philip H. Sheridan who had died in 1888. Afterwards his widow felt she must live near his memorial, so she sold her residence on Rhode Island Avenue and built 2211 Massachusetts for herself and two daughters. (It is now owned by the Greek Embassy nearby.) This balcony *(see opposite)* was added outside her upper windows so that she could step out and see the Memorial.

Gutzom Borglum's statue of Sheridan, unveiled November 26, 1908, is a unique equestrian monument. It was not placed high on a pedestal, but only three feet off the ground. The pose of the horse was a "snapshot" of one stirring moment. Shown here one and three-quarters his actual size, this magnificent animal was of Black Hawk blood and presented to the General in 1862 by officers of the Second Michigan Cavalry in Rienzi, Mississippi. Its coolness under fire, stamina, and intelligence, while ridden by Sheridan through forty-eight engagements and battles, became legendary.

The moment which Borglum chose to immor-

talize was on October 19, 1864, when Sheridan, warned that General Jubal Early's Confederates were unexpectedly about to defeat his troops encamped at Cedar Creek near Winchester, Virginia, galloped back the twenty miles through the night from Winchester to cheer on his men. He checks "Rienzi" suddenly so that the horse falls back on his haunches and stiffens his forelegs to retain balance, while "Little Phil" whips off his hat in response to his cheering and later victorious regiment. The horse then became known as "Winchester."

Reaction to this startling pose was variable.

One critic said "Winchester" looked stuck in Cedar Creek mud. Another remarked that the chaotic intermingling of horse-drawn carriages and the backfiring, horseless vehicles just coming into use needed Sheridan's direction. But the majority showed enthusiasm for the statue of the bold leader shown here in his prime at thirty-three years old. President Theodore Roosevelt gave Lt. Philip H. Sheridan, Jr. leave from the Army to pose for the sculptor in his father's uniform and hat and on his Mexican saddle with authentic bridle and trappings.

Looking up R Street past where Chief Justice Charles Evans Hughes lived from 1923 to 1932. Notice the porte-cocheres. Made of glass and wrought iron, this amalgam would be impossible today. Charles Francis Adams, Secretary of the Navy in Herbert Hoover's cabinet, entered and departed under the third one.

Beginning at the corner of Decatur Place are three embassies, that of Pakistan at 2315 Massachusetts, the Republic of China at 2311, and that of Chile at 2305. 2315 shows George Oakley Totten, Jr., architect, at his Beaux Arts best. The rounded turret reminiscent of the Hotel Negresco in Nice, the detail of the narrow bas reliefs catching the sun, and the balcony outside the Ambassador's office-windows contribute to an especially pleasant stroll.

Kalorama, the old estate for which this area is named, has many houses built in the Twenties after World War I, and used now for Embassies, workshops, studios, museums and chanceries. Here at 2301 S Street is a workshop for fine silkscreen print-making, with emphasis on the procedure, care and maintenance of high quality prints.

Opposite: Here is a courtyard just a few yards off Massachusetts. The decor surrounding the fountain in the Islamic Center is in the traditional Moslem ornamental style, that is, it does not represent human beings or animals, but is styled on plant or abstract forms.

In 1966 the English-Speaking Union placed this bronze statue of Sir Winston Churchill on the sidewalk in front of the British Embassy. The big question had been: What should he wear? The British wanted him in either the boiler suit or the traditional garb of the Order of the Garter. The Americans felt he should be familiarly presented in a business suit with the V-sign, walking stick, and cigar. Some objected he would look as if flagging a cab. Others said the cigar would be vandalized and look undignified. The cigar manufacturers wrote insisting on this controversial point. The American version was decided upon. Churchill's dual citizenship was represented by placing the left foot on British Embassy soil, the front foot on that of the District of Columbia, and the walking stick on the dividing line. The sculptor was William McVey.

Opposite: The Washington National Cathedral after a Christmas blizzard.

Perhaps of all residential areas in Washington, Cleveland Park most typically
represents turn-of-the-century middle-America. Its houses have wide front porches,
cupolas, front yards and garden borders. The area took its name when President
Grover Cleveland bought one of its homes in 1885 for a summer residence, tore it
down and replaced it with the kind of roomy house like those he had been used to in
Buffalo, New York.

Battery Kemble Park, located at a strategically high spot between Loughboro and Foxall Roads, held a battery guarding the environs of the City near Chain Bridge during the Civil War.

Atlas and his twin support the pillars of the entrance to the Reptile House at the Zoo. The National Zoological Park, under the direction of the Smithsonian Institution, occupies a scenic location, which drops down a ravine 220 feet to Rock Creek.

4 *From Dupont Circle to Sixteenth Street and east to the National Arboretum ...*

A tranquil moment at Dupont Circle around
I I :30 A.M. before noon rush hour begins.

Looking across the Circle you see one of the few turn-of-the-century mansions still left in the area. Built by Mr. and Mrs. Herbert Wadsworth as a winter residence, it is now the Sulgrave Club, exclusively for women.

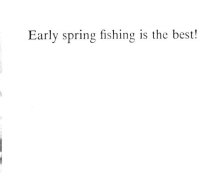
Early spring fishing is the best!

Saturday afternoon at the fountain.

This unusual building at 1526 New Hampshire Avenue was erected by Mrs. William C. Whittemore in 1892, and has found a lively and popular destiny as the Women's National Democratic Club, which bought it in 1927. Its wedge-like design shows how the discipline of these triangular lots you find all over Washington can challenge an architect, in this case, Harvey Page.

A capital on the porch of the old Panamanian Embassy
built in 1891 at 1533 New Hampshire Avenue.

Visitors often mention the capital's unusually "green" look and its beautiful trees. A vista in early spring up New Hampshire Avenue toward Dupont Circle not only illustrates this but also the light, airy look distinguishing many of the wide Avenues. After much trial and error, the District discovered the kind of trees which thrive here, whose roots go deep and do not crack pavements or raise curbs and sidewalks.

But more than expert tree-care has brought this about. Washington has a low profile. Because buildings are kept low, light can flood the streets, trees grow tall and leaf out, then arch gracefully. How did this happen? From reading his "Note" of November 30, 1790, and "Opinion" of March 11, 1791, sent to George Washington during the early planning-phase of the capital before L'Enfant began his survey, it is evident that Thomas Jefferson generated the idea of the "low profile." He had an analytical, practical mind combined with a highly developed artistic sense, and after five years in Paris, had made cogent observations.

"In Paris it is forbidden," he wrote Washington, "to build a house beyond a given height, & it is admitted to be a good reservation, it keeps the houses low & convenient, and the streets light and airy, fires are much more manageable where streets are low." Although one who viewed city life with distaste, he now turned with gusto and conviction to building a capital from scratch. Building regulations declared by the President October 17, 1791, reflected his opinions. When the three Commissioners met with builders, they enforced these regulations, and the trend was set.

The zest of these lads playing on the derelict brownstone gates at the corner of Florida Avenue and Sixteenth matches that of the remarkable woman who built them. Mary Foote Henderson was the wife of John B. Henderson, Senator from Missouri 1826–69. In 1888 as the boundaries of the City were extended and Sixteenth was paved with cobblestones, the Hendersons, who had retired to St. Louis, returned to the capital and built on this 8-acre site a grotesque Rhenish, red sandstone castle with five or six tiers of windows and a turret resembling the setting for a Gothic romance.

In 1913 she prevailed on Congress to rename Sixteenth the "Avenue of the Presidents." Her satisfaction was short-lived. A year later Congress voted by amendment that Sixteenth Street should be named that forever, and that was that.

That year her husband died, and immediately afterwards, the gutters of Sixteenth ran red with wines from his well-stocked cellars. Teetotaler, vegetarian, crusader against the demons of rum and nicotine, even short skirts, this ardent reformer and "Queen Mary" as Washington hostesses called her, died in 1931.

The building was torn down in 1949, and the site has been sold to the National Baptist Church for a housing complex and nursing home.

Finished in 1940, Meridian Hill Park is the City's only formal public park in the European tradition. (Malcolm X Park is now its local name.) The site was first called Meridian Hill in 1820 by a sailor, Commodore David Porter, who with prize money from fighting Barbary pirates bought 110 acres of the Hill on which to build a handsome brick mansion. In 1829 John Quincy Adams retired here. He never could resist using a spyglass to discern his bitter rival and successor, Andrew Jackson, mount his horse under the new North Porch of the White House and ride off to the Capitol. The house burned in 1863.

Fifty years later "Queen Mary" Henderson purchased the property for $120,680, and then wanted to give it to the City as Henderson Park. In 1912 Congress authorized its sale to the government tax-free for $490,000, but refused to attach her name, pointing out the 400% profit she had made on the deal was recompense enough.

The cascade of thirteen falls dramatizes a decisive feature of the city's design. A rim of hills, beginning above Georgetown and representing the drop from the Piedmont plateau to the coastal plain, encircles Washington on the north. Exploring the virgin landscape in March 1791, L'Enfant with his engineer's eye must have noted the defense potential in this high commanding ring, and so planned the urban grid to cover the plain and stop at the natural rise of terrain.

A game of catch goes on behind the back of Francis Asbury, the Methodist circuit-riding preacher who was called "Prophet of the Long Road." He looks down Sixteenth Street, a Maryland commuter's long road home.

The Jeanne d'Arc, reproduction of the famous original by Paul Dubois in front of Rheims Cathedral and the only equestrienne statue in Washington, was presented "Aux Femmes d'Amerique" by the Franco-American Société de Femmes de France à New York.

In August 1861, Fort Massachusetts, renamed Fort Stevens after General Isaac Stevens who fell at Bull Run I, was constructed at what is now Quackenbos Avenue and 13th Street as one of forty-eight forts which ringed Washington. The only time the Confederate Army penetrated this ring was on July 12, 1864, when General Jubal Early advanced through Silver Spring, Maryland, and to within shooting distance of Fort Stevens. Grant was besieging Petersburg, near Richmond, and Early hoped to draw the Union Army forces away from the Confederate capital. He did so, panicking Washington residents. Noting a conspicuous gap in the defending Confederate front, Grant dispatched the Sixth Corps up the Potomac to Washington.

Arriving at the Seventh Street wharves, they were greeted by President Abraham Lincoln, who was anxious to view a battle and rode with the army out the Seventh Street Road to the Fort. By this time Early's cavalry had attacked from the east, infantry was skirmishing around firing their guns, and in order to get a better view, the fearless President in his stovepipe hat climbed a parapet above where the boy is crouching in the picture. Behind him he heard a shout. "Get down, you fool! You'll be shot." He did, and in a hurry. The speaker was Lt. Oliver Wendell Holmes of Boston, Massachusetts, later Associate Justice of the United States Supreme Court, and aide to the commandant of the Sixth Corps. The Confederates soon retired, because as Early later disclosed in his Memoirs, their every move could be discerned and signalled by the Signal Corps wigwagging atop Scott Tower at the United States Soldiers' Home.

These benches lead up to Anderson Cottage, called "Corn Rigs" by its first owner, George W. Riggs, who with W. W. Corcoran founded the Riggs National Bank. He did not name his country estate for himself but for the Scottish word "rig," meaning ridge or furrow and alluding to the cornfields on the estate. At the insistence of General Winfield Scott, who led American forces in the Mexican War, Congress allotted part of the tribute money Scott received in 1848 from General Santa Anna, to buy the Riggs estate of about 255 acres for a Soldiers' Home. Lincoln spent several summers here, four miles from the White House and much higher and cooler. In July of 1862 he drafted the Emancipation Proclamation in its parlor. At his suggestion the Cottage was renamed for Major Robert Anderson who commanded Fort Sumter, South Carolina, when the first Confederate shot was fired on it, beginning the Civil War.

In the background rises Scott Tower where the Signal Corps wigwagged information about Jubal Early's maneuvers. Why one minaret is taller than the others has always puzzled the Home's research staff. The first tower of 1859 had no minarets; then around 1874 it was given a Mansard turret. About 1890 this was removed and replaced by the present one. It could be, said one researcher, that with the Washington monument just completed, some builder had the mistaken notion that he could top it, and so added an extra stake and ball to the minaret facing the Monument. The Scott Tower is 350 feet high, and the Monument, 555 feet high.

Through the gazebo near the Home's hospital,
you see the green on the second hole of the
golf course laid out on the old Riggs estate.

Early morning reflections of Howard University in the McMillan Reservoir.

Left: High on a Georgia Avenue hill, near the predominantly Black University he founded, stands the still handsome house of Major General Oliver Otis Howard, West-Pointer and Civil War veteran in charge of Federal funds for establishing Negro schools through the Freedmen's Bureau after the Civil War. When he was a child in Maine, his father had brought home to the farm a Negro lad who had lived and worked and played with Otis for four years. The General later attributed his freedom from racial prejudice to this "providential circumstance." While chartered by Congress in 1867 as a school for training ministers, Howard quickly expanded its curriculum, and today is an outstanding Black national university with ten thousand students in its undergraduate and graduate schools, including many East Indian, African, and West Indian students. Now over a century old, the mansion is still proud and significant but deteriorating. Alumni sentiment refuses to allow it to be razed, and the new buildings for Administration (to the left) and Social Work (to right) have been built around it.

Left, below: While standing on a lawn on the lower quadrangle to photograph the handsome clock-tower, a group of young men sauntered over to ask what I was doing. I explained I was working on a photo-essay of historic Washington. "What about Fourteenth Street? You goin' to photograph that? That's historic." "No," I answered. "There were other Fourteenth Streets. There was Watts and Detroit. . . I'm not doing a social document. . . This is historic Washington, and Howard was important to the story. It's one of the oldest educational institutions here." For a few seconds, silence. Then this student moved in close. "Take my picture," he said. "Okay," I answered and did so, grateful for what I saw as understanding and pride in his attitude. After that, the men walked away chuckling, no doubt amused by the whims of lady photographers, but leaving me with an anecdote that clarified better than any explanation the focus of this book.

William Battle painted this mural of Afro-Americans in the theatre on the south wall of the Ira Aldridge Theatre at Howard. It is one of five painted by student-artists on various exterior walls of the campus as a project for 1969–70 conceived in a spirit of Black pride.

An old Black neighborhood near Howard
built about the same time as Cleveland Park.

In 1712 the first services recorded in what became the District of Columbia were held near what is now St. Paul's Church on Rock Creek Church Road, possibly under a great tree, called the Glebe Oak, said to be over five hundred years old, and just out of the picture to the right.

The congregation has passed through an agonizing but firm integration. Black communicants now represent one-fifth of the congregation; two vestrymen are Black; and Blacks are now buried in the historic cemetery where many Colonial and Federal ancestors of contemporary Washington residents are also buried.

Right: Down a slope east of St. Paul's Church and back from the gravelled road, stands a separate grove of thick evergreen and holly. Inside before a semicircular bench, sits a mysterious and shrouded bronze figure, unnamed and without inscription. It is the memorial Henry Adams, native of Boston, but resident and lover of Washington since before the Civil War, commissioned the sculptor Auguste St. Gaudens to create over the grave of his wife, Marian, a tragic suicide in 1885. Adams soon departed on a long journey to the South Seas. Never telling the sculptor what he wanted, he even refused to see the figure in clay. His only stipulation was to the architect of the pedestal and bench, Stanford White. He asked that whatever was placed back of the figure should have nothing to say, and above all, not be classic.

After returning to Washington, he went at once to view the memorial. Here at last he had found the solace long sought on his lonely travels. Calling it "The Peace of God," he said in his autobiography, *The Education of Henry Adams,* that "the interest of the figure is not its meaning, but in the response of the observer." A remark attributed to Mark Twain, however, that the enigmatic figure embodied all human grief, led to its being known generally as "Grief." This is how you will find it identified today in Washington guidebooks.

Opposite: Photographed through an arch of McMahon Hall at Catholic University, the symbols of Our Lady laid in brilliant tiles, the Fleur de Lys, the Star of the Sea, and the Tower of Ivory glisten on the great azure dome of the Shrine of the Immaculate Conception built during the late 1950s at the corner of Harewood Road and Michigan Avenue NE. With its chapels and accommodations for around six thousand worshippers, the Shrine is the national center for Roman Catholic worship.

The deaf of America presented this charming group by Daniel Chester French to Gallaudet College of the Deaf at the eastern terminus of Florida Avenue NE. It shows the world-famous teacher of the deaf, Dr. Thomas Hopkins Gallaudet, showing a young student how to fingerspell the letter A.

Using the language of signs and fingerspelling in all academic departments and throughout its daily life, this unique institution was authorized by President Abraham Lincoln in 1864 to confer degrees in liberal arts and sciences. Numbering around one thousand, the student body contains many people from all over the world, and a Gallaudet graduate is distinguished by a rare determination and drive.

It is interesting that it took a Gallaudet team to invent the football huddle. Around 1885 the College was playing Yale at Gallaudet, and afraid the Yalie scouts had learned enough signs to understand their signals, the Gallaudet team invented the huddle to keep their moves secret.

At 14th and Quincy Streets NE is the Franciscan Monastery noted not only for its similarity to the cloisters at Assisi in the Tuscan Hills, but also its famous roses. With bushes sometimes four and five feet high, they represent many varieties and are at their height in late May.

Around the first of May drifts of dogwood in bloom at the National Arboretum make a stroll along its paths a memorable experience. The Arboretum is just a few minutes drive from Gallaudet off Bladensburg Road NE. It was down this Road at twilight August 24, 1814, that the triumphant, red-coated 21st Foot of Wellington's Invincibles marched into Washington to burn the Capitol.

5 *Capitol Hill*

Washington's Diary, March 29, 1791: "In a thick mist, and under strong appearance of rain, (which however did not happen) I set out about 7 o'clock . . ." to examine the ground himself where L'Enfant wanted to place the Capitol building. Taken March 18, 1970, this photograph shows that at least one aspect of the Federal City has not changed, namely March weather, and that a class of boys is also setting out to examine the Capitol.

Latrobe designed the capitals and dome over the small Senate Rotunda to show tobacco flowers and leaves *(above, left),* indicating the importance of this plant in the young nation's economy. He had the task of repairing the Capitol after the British burned it in 1814, and designed this rotunda as a light well to replace some burned-out stairs.

Latrobe's "Corn-cob capitals"

Opposite: The dome in a rain-puddle.

Two young Swiss visitors frame L'Enfant's dream, the broad green Mall leading down to a monument to George Washington. In the foreground, in silhouette, is the Grant Memorial; beyond the Monument, the Lincoln Memorial lights have just this moment been illuminated.

John Marshall, fourth Chief Justice of the United States Supreme Court, sits on the west terrace with his back to the Dome. Some say this symbolizes how he established the independence of the Judiciary Branch from the Legislative and the Executive.

Washington could well be called the City of Fountains. When it was first surveyed, twenty-eight natural springs were discovered in the District. This drinking fountain at the bottom of the west terrace, one of the Olmsted designs, is on the site of one of these natural springs.

x

Looking straight down Maryland Avenue SW past the Garfield Statue to the HEW
Building. Landscape architect Frederick Law Olmsted of New York City, designer of
Central Park in New York City, came to Washington in 1874 to spend eleven years
designing the grounds of Capitol Hill. His assistant, Thomas Widedell, designed
these handsome terraces, stairways, and the architectural detail, even the gutters
crisscrossing the lower platforms.

Union Cavalry charge at the Grant Memorial.

In 1877 Congress purchased this fountain by Frederic Auguste Bartholdi from the French artist after it was exhibited at the Philadelphia Centennial of 1876. The fountain stands in the grounds of the Botanic Garden whose conservatory looms in the background.

Opposite: White magnolias in early bloom against the cupola and dome of the Library of Congress.

What student in Washington for a holiday and with a term-paper to write, doesn't know the simultaneous tedium and sense of awe while waiting at a seat in this grand circle of the Reading Room for his books? His call-slips will probably be returned "Not On Shelf."

The Monocle, 107 D Street NE, on the Senate side of the Hill has many guests from that part of the Capitol. The gaslight chandelier over the bar is original with this antebellum building. The mural on the second floor of the Monocle *(see bottom)* is painted so that no matter where you stand or sit, the street leading up to the Capitol is in perspective.

The Museum of African Art is located at 316–18 A Street NE in the first Washington home of Frederick Douglass, the ex-slave who served in high government posts under Presidents Grant through Cleveland. He lived here from 1871 to 1877. His second and last home here was on Cedar Hill, Anacostia, shown later in the book.

The Museum has permanent and changing exhibits for an ever-changing audience. *Above, left:* Sculptures of two life-size ancestor figures of the Ibo people of Nigeria (The de Havenon Collection). *Above, right:* A wrought-iron sculpture group of the Bambara and Dogon peoples of Mali.

On the steps of the United States Supreme Court building, against a forest of Corinthian capitals, this massive female figure ponders the problems of justice as she holds a small model of a figure of Justice in her right hand, a pigeon in her lap, and a book of laws in her left hand.

Three great law-givers of the Eastern and Mediterranean civilizations, Moses,
Confucius, and Solon, look down from the East pediment of the Supreme Court,
right into one of residential Capitol Hill's restored alleys off A Street NE.

6 From the residential Hill to Anacostia, and back to Southwest Washington ...

Looking past the marvelous mixture of objects in the window of Antiques-on-the-Hill, you see Eastern Market which, like the market of any small town, is a center for Hill activity, especially on Saturday mornings, winter or summer.

The Eastern Market.

Roofline watchers, used to residential Capitol Hill's rows of brick dwellings built in the Eighties, will look twice at this break in the pattern, a gray cottage of 1840 in the bracketed style at 616 North Carolina Avenue SE. Opposite the Eastern Market, it was built by Lucretia Parsons who held the entire block until 1865 and ran it as a farm. Few antebellum residences like the Parsons house remain to suggest how rural was the landscape in that era.

Here is a town within a town, the way it was in the Jeffersonian era when legislators lived up here in boardinghouses, inns and rented rooms. Today, restored houses painted in contrasting hues, gaudy pink next to pastel green, rub shoulders with unrestored shabby bricks and rambling frames. Librarians en route to work with rare incunabula at the Folger Library or scholars to the Smithsonian pass vagrants.

Signs like this could have been found in many boardinghouses near the Capitol as early as the Jeffersonian era. At that time Washington was composed of two villages, legislative and executive. Congressmen and for the most part senators, too, lived on the Hill and ate at "messes" which usually represented a homogeneous political front. To reach the executive area around the White House, they had to cross a creek and wade through swamps. The Supreme Court, the judicial branch, served justice in the basement of the Capitol.

Grillework on the rear garden and windows
of a house fronting on New Jersey.

Opposite: A sidewalk of New Jersey Avenue SE, one of early
Washington's most historic and populated avenues. The building
beyond the two friends is the Longworth House Office Building, at the
northwest corner of C and New Jersey. In 1800, November 26, when
Thomas Jefferson arrived to stay until his inauguration as President
four months later, this site was occupied by Conrad and McNunn's
famous boardinghouse and "mess." New Jersey starts at the Navy
Yard and was the road by which all manner of materials, statuary,
furnishings and equipment for the Capitol was hauled up to the Hill
until railroads came into the area in the 1850s.

In spring of 1801 President Thomas Jefferson and Lt. Col. Commandant Burrows of the United States Marine Corps rode together around Capitol Hill searching for a proper site for the Barracks near the Navy Yard and the Capitol. They chose Square 927 at Eighth and I Streets, SE (now just north of the Southwest Freeway), and on June 20 the government paid the original proprietor William Prout 4 cents per square foot for the two-block site.

Built in 1805, the Commandant's house is the oldest public building in continuous use in Washington. The White House could not qualify for this distinction because after the British burned it August 24, 1814, it did not reopen until President and Mrs. James Monroe gave a reception New Year's Day, 1818. The present barracks are not original, but were rebuilt in 1901.

Photographed at twilight, this charming little Gothic Revival church has the air of an English country village church, and indeed it was designed in 1805 by an English architect, Benjamin Henry Latrobe.

It was often attended by Thomas Jefferson who was widely regarded, to quote *The Washington Guidebook,* as an agnostic. On his way to church one day a doubter stopped him to ask why he was going, since "you do not believe a word of it." Jefferson replied, "Sir, no nation has yet existed or been governed without religion. I, as the chief magistrate of this nation, am bound to give it the sanction of my example. Good morning, Sir."

Opened in 1807 and turned over to Christ Church in 1812, this Cemetery was intended primarily for Congressmen and Senators too far away from home to be transported there for burial. Senator George Hoar of Massachusetts is said to have declared that being buried under one of these cenotaphs, or tea caddies as they were colloquially called, would add a new terror to death. Altogether over 80,000 people are buried here, some in mass graves, and you can come across all manner of people, ranging from Chief of the Choctaws Push-Ma Ta-Ha who died of croup at the age of sixty, to John Philip Sousa who died in 1932.

Across the Eastern Branch you can drive up Martin Luther King Jr. Avenue, and encounter the high brick walls of St. Elizabeth's Hospital. Driving inside and around the tennis courts to the terrace turn-around, you find an incomparable view of Washington, and especially the juncture of the Eastern Branch or Anacostia River with the Washington Channel, and beyond East Potomac Park, the Potomac River.

Old houses of the Eighties bowered in June roses.

Cedar Hill, where Frederick Douglass lived from 1877 to his death in 1895, is a
national Black shrine. Born a slave in Talbot County on Maryland's Eastern Shore,
he was self-educated, and at the age of twenty escaped slavery to become a leading
abolitionist newspaperman. Writer, orator, and proponent of women's rights
as well, he became minister to Haiti, the first Black U.S. Marshal, and the D.C.
Recorder of Deeds.

Included in the District of Columbia at the instance of Thomas Jefferson in 1791,
Anacostia today is a Black community of 196,500 people. But when Cedar Hill was
built before the Civil War, the initial settlement was a small subdivision called
Uniontown where white slave-owning planters and merchants lived. After Douglass'
death, one poet wrote: "Howl, fir-tree, for the Cedar of Lebanon has fallen."

Above: Carrollsburg Place is the only street in Washington named for the original settlement on Greenleaf's Point belonging to Daniel Carroll before 1791.

Right: Between 1794–1796 James Greenleaf built several substantial brick houses on this point, believing it would become the primary trading center of the new city. Thomas Law brought his bride to this one on the waterfront. She was the granddaughter of Martha Washington. Now well restored, it is used by the de luxe Southwest Renewal apartment complex as a kind of clubhouse.

The history of the Washington Navy Yard, whose site was selected by George Washington himself, began when President John Adams completed the original purchase of land October 2, 1799. You can enter through the Latrobe Gate at 8th and M Streets, SE, and see the first commandant's house built in 1804, that of Captain Thomas Tingey. Then wander into Leutze Park to inspect curious foreign cannon captured in American naval battles all over the world. Walking downhill, you reach the waterfront where an intriguing array of old cannon and nautical armament face the placid Eastern Branch. In the Museum you'll find dioramas of famous naval battles, that of the *Bonhomme Richard* vs. the *Serapis,* for example, where John Paul Jones cried: "We have not yet begun to fight!" The Yard has survived many stirring moments, all told vividly in an excellent booklet,

A Historic Heritage, by Katherine Ainsworth Semmes, sold for $1.00 at the Museum.

Between 1806 and 1879 twenty-two ships for the United States Navy were built here, and afterwards, the Yard continued making naval ordnance until 1961. Today it functions as headquarters for Naval District, Washington, D.C., supervising over one hundred naval activities in the Metro-Washington area, Maryland and Virginia.

This red ship berthed here belongs to the National Capital Parks Service. The man taking his quiet lunch-break works in the "Lightship's" hull preparing tanks for marine specimens to be exhibited later at Hains Point as part of an environmental education center. In the background is the Frederick Douglass Bridge, leading from South Capitol Street to Anacostia and Suitland.

Across the tennis courts is an old brick house which during the Civil War was a penitentiary. Here in the northeast bedroom on the second floor, were tried four of the conspirators of the Lincoln assassination plot, Mrs. Mary Surratt, George A. Atzerodt, David E. Herold, and Lewis Payne. The wall near these tennis courts was close by the gallows on which they were hanged. It is believed the bodies were buried near the practice board in the picture. (It should be said that years later the innocence of Mrs. Surratt was irrefutably established.)

General officers' quarters at Fort McNair, all alike, face onto the
parade ground, at south end of which stands the Army War College.

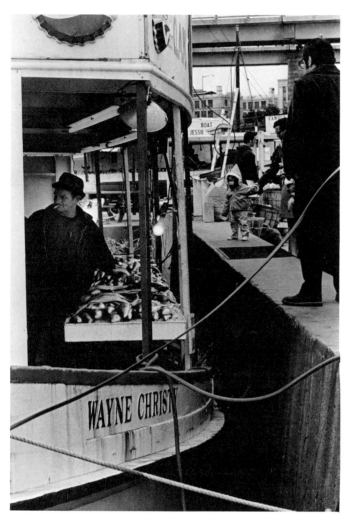

For a long time this stretch
along the waterfront near the
bridge and off Maine Avenue
has held a fish market.

Looking across Washington Channel, you see the general officers'
quarters again, still marching along regular as soldiers.

7 *From the Tidal Basin to midtown Washington, and finally, the Washington Monument . . .*

A sunny, warmish Saturday afternoon in early March. Where'll we go, left to the Jefferson Memorial, or right around the Basin? The gulls in the center don't care. At last the ice is out, and they can float happily on the sparkling water.

The outstanding feature of this bronze statue of Thomas Jefferson is its height of 19′, 6″. Measuring 6′, 2″ himself, and with a figure "straight as a gun barrel," Jefferson's stature was always an impressive aspect of his presence. Shown as he looked during his presidency, 1801–1809, his face wears the benign, unruffled expression often observed by his visitors.

Another feature is the robe Jefferson wears, trimmed with rich furs presented to him in 1798 in Philadelphia by the Polish patriot, Thaddeus Kosciuszko, who had received them the year before from Czar Paul I of Russia. Jefferson had the coat made of plum-colored wool lined with flannel and cross-stitched with his initials and wore it all his life afterwards. The long fur-piece still remains in the hands of a direct descendant living in Charlottesville, Virginia.

The sculptor, Rudolph Evans, had seen the Virginian wearing it in a portrait in the United States Military Academy, which was founded by Jefferson in 1801. The Academy had commissioned Thomas Sully to paint Jefferson in 1822 at Monticello.

For the sculptor the robe solved two problems: it provided a unified composition and prevented visitors from seeing each other through the legs of the statue.

These fishermen are more in tune with the past than they may know or care, or than the other cherry blossom fans to the right. Throughout the nineteenth century the Tidal Basin formed part of the mouth of Tiber Creek until the latter was walled in around 1911. In the spring, herring abounded here. Despite today's pollution these boys, like all true fishermen, have brought a bag big enough for the catch their forebears would have made a century ago.

Constitution Avenue overlays the old Washington Canal constructed in the early 1800s in the bed of Tiber Creek, a tidal estuary whose mouth was where the Lincoln Memorial is now. Connecting Georgetown with Washington, it was intended to bring trade into the capital from Maryland and Virginia. In part, particularly after the C & O Canal was finished, it did accomplish this. The red sandstone blocks, for example, from which the old towered Smithsonian was built in 1848, were brought by barge from Seneca, Maryland, down this canal.

But problems multiplied. Financing dragged. Tidal silt clogged the waterway so that shipping dwindled. Nine sewers drained into it, and it was not uncommon to find cows, drunks, and small children mired down in its muck. All combined to make the swampy area around the present Monument grounds a stinking health menace. To remedy this, A. R. Shepherd and his Board of Public Works in 1873 laid culverts and filled the Canal to make a road of sorts called B Street. But this only served to render a turbulent region more so.

During the Civil War crowds of emancipated Negroes built a shantytown along the Canal between Eleventh and Fifteenth Streets which was soon labeled Murder Bay. After B Street opened up, the Bay flourished with a red light district, gin mills and gambling dens. Until 1930 when the Federal Triangle replaced it and B became Constitution Avenue, a rowdy yet furtive atmosphere prevailed. Nothing remains today to suggest a rich tradition which enlivened central Washington life for over sixty years.

The towers of the old Smithsonian Institution designed by
James Renwick in 1848 dominate the Mall on the south side.

Some of Washington's outdoor sculpture is spectacular. Here is
an Alexander Calder outside the Smithsonian's attractive cafeteria.

Washington has over two hundred diverse memorials. Some reaffirm the city's history, its personality, and the people's taste. Others are embarrassing. Here is one of the latter with, however, a saga worth the telling.

To commemorate the centennial of George Washington's birth in 1835, Congress commissioned the sculptor Horatio Greenough to carve a statue of the President for the Capitol Rotunda. Being a classicist, Greenough felt compelled to do this in Florence, Italy, and like Michelangelo, use Carrara marble. After dedicating nine years to his work, he finished in 1841 and shipped the statue to the Washington Navy Yard.

In sweltering August heat the fourteen-ton bulk was dragged up New Jersey Avenue and the Capitol's east front steps to the main doorway. Here it proved too big to pass through, and masonry was taken down to provide entrance-room. Placed in the center of the Rotunda and unveiled, it caused immediate consternation. Nobody had thought to ask the sculptor for a preliminary sketch. Now here was the Father of our Country shown not as a great general or president, but as a Roman Senator, a Zeus, with only a toga resembling a bath towel to cover his nudity.

Many amusing comments were made. One critic later wrote that his hands indicated: "My body is at Mount Vernon, my clothes at the Patent Office." Moreover, the tremendous weight threatened the Rotunda floor. So within the year, masonry at the front door was again taken down, and the statue lowered down the steps to be placed on the East Capitol plaza.

Here it remained (sheltered by a shed) until 1908. During the celebration over Admiral Dewey's return from the Philippines October 6, 1899, the shed was removed. People clambered over the statue, hung onto its arms and sat on its head, drumming heels on the broad chest in time to the Marine Band's music. At length it was banished to a remote corner of the Smithsonian among antique printing-presses. Graffiti soon appeared on it like: "Hi, toots" and "Keep your shirt on."

At last the marble Washington achieved a place of honor when the Museum of History and Technology was built. He was placed near the flag Francis Scott Key saw waving at dawn in 1814 when he wrote the "Star-Spangled Banner."

Gilbert Stuart painted this portrait of George Washington, called the Vaughan Portrait, from life in 1795. It comes from the Andrew Mellon Collection at the National Gallery. Here is how the President looked when he often visited the growing Federal City to work with L'Enfant, deal with the original proprietors of the land in the District of Columbia, and as he laid the cornerstone of the Capitol's north wing on July 4, 1793.

Some handsome business façades from 1011 to 1021 7th Street, NW, built between 1870 and 1890. At 1021, H. Ruppert built his hardware store in 1890. W. Ruppert, representing the fourth generation, is in the same business there today.

The Old Patent Office, Washington's third oldest building, at 9th and G Streets NW, has found a new and distinguished destiny under the Smithsonian umbrella as the National Portrait Gallery and the National Collection of Fine Arts. Begun in 1836, it was finished after the Civil War.

The Lincoln Gallery in the Old Patent Office, an amazingly light, airy hall, with marble pillars and pleasing arches, was the scene of Abraham Lincoln's second inaugural ball. While the 4,000 guests promenaded, they looked at patent models displayed in sidewall cases.

Above: Does the proprietor of 604 H Street NW in Washington's Chinatown, the Suey Lang Lung Company, know that he operates out of an historic building? Freshly painted a neat white, this antebellum house looks more presentable than it did in 1865 when it vibrated with the furtive activities of John Wilkes Booth's shabby group of conspirators plotting the assassination of Abraham Lincoln. This was the boardinghouse of Mrs. Mary E. Jenkins Surratt.

Right: Afraid that the cobblestoned drive back to the White House might prove fatal to the President, a doctor ordered him carried across the street to this house belonging to a Swedish tailor named William Pedersen. He died the next morning in a little backroom at 7:22 A.M.

The Ford Theatre at 511 10th Street NW has been restored to look today the way it did on the fatal night of April 14, 1865, Good Friday, when Lincoln was shot, and Booth leapt from the box onto the stage, shouting "Sic Semper Tyrannis" (Ever Thus To Tyrants), and escaped out a rear door.

The Ben Franklin Post Office clocktower stands up like a Romanesque landmark to locate this pleasant street café on the Pennsylvania Avenue Plaza. Bassin's clientele comes mostly from Commerce, Labor, and the District Building across the Plaza, the Treasury to the west, and from the National Press Building just north up the hill on 14th Street.

This prim and proper statue of Ben Franklin on a little plaza at 10th and Pennsylvania should by rights make a quarter-turn to the west. Then he would face the old post office and clocktower named for him only a block down The Avenue. As it is, he demonstrates his magnetism for the indomitable birds whose ancestors may well have been part of his postal system. They certainly feel at home with him.

Overleaf: The first 150′ of the Monument were built between 1848 and 1855, then left open to the weather, while the Civil War was fought and the nation partially recovered. Work resumed in 1880 and it was finished 1884. During the building, 190 tribute stones from all manner of groups, states, territories, citizens of foreign countries, Volunteer Fire Departments, Temperance organizations, the Red Men of America, stones in Welsh, Greek and Chinese, were built into the walls. The National Park Service administering the Monument does not allow you to walk up. So you have to walk down the 898 steps, a hike well worth it, to inspect one of Washington's most fascinating historic sights.

PRESENTED BY THE FIRE DEPARTMENT
OF PHILADELPHIA.
1854.

DESERET

DESERET
MEANS HONEY BEE
CHANGED TO
TERRITORY OF UTAH 1850
STATE OF UTAH 1896

Whether Amish or Mennonite, this writer never discovered.
But evidently they can't wait to get to the top of the Monument.